STANLEY GIBBONS GUIDES

COLLECTING MILITARY MEDALS AND DECORATIONS

David Paterson

STANLEY GIBBONS PUBLICATIONS LTD

391 Strand, London WC2R 0LX

By Appointment to Her Majesty The Queen
Stanley Gibbons Ltd, London
Philatelists

Set in 8 on 9pt Monotype Century Schoolbook and
printed in Great Britain by Waterlow (Dunstable) Ltd.

Contents

The Author

David Paterson's interest in the subject began in 1941 in South Africa where, as a small boy, he collected a wartime series of cigarette cards featuring war medals. A serious collector since 1970, he now concentrates on early medal books. Mr. Paterson joined the Stanley Gibbons Group in 1969 and has been with Stanley Gibbons Currency Ltd. since 1972. He helped to set up the War Medal Department of that Company in 1977 and the steady expansion of this part of the business led to the opening of its own premises in Piccadilly Arcade in June 1979.

Introduction

Military medal collecting has always been popular among those interested in militaria, and this has been particularly noticeable in the last few years. Apart from the advantage of taking up less space than other forms of military collecting— such as uniforms, swords and firearms—most medals, especially the British issues, have the bonus of bearing the recipient's name and regiment or ship. This gives the hobby its very personal attraction, as the man to whom the medal was issued becomes of immediate interest to the collector and historian. Records can be studied, military and regimental histories referred to, and by this research the story of an individual soldier's military life unfolds. It is also sometimes possible to obtain photographs and service documents which add to the story.

The growing interest in medals has also been reflected in the steady increase in the price of these items, especially during the 1970s. This is particularly so for pre-1900 campaign medals and most decorations, though there is still the odd bargain to be had from all periods, especially with the post-1900 issues. Decorations for bravery are much in demand, as many of these have fascinating details of the award. Foreign medals have also gained in popularity; unfortunately most of these are unnamed, but a very colourful collection can be made from these most attractive awards. Another important factor is that, apart from the historical interest, military medals have proved to be a very good financial investment in the past, and there is no reason to suppose that this will not continue.

Awards for military service and for gallantry in battle have been known for a very considerable time. An early example is the Greek *ta phalara*, later adopted by the Romans as the *phalerae*: these were circular breast ornaments worn by soldiers on armoured helmets or breast plates (Fig.1). During the Middle Ages in Europe grateful rulers presented their followers with suits of armour, inscribed swords and other weapons as tokens of their appreciation for acts of military gallantry. The European Renaissance period produced a number of artists who struck medallions to commemorate battles and military victories and the practice spread to England, particularly following the reign of King Henry VIII (1509-47).

Great Britain to 1837

Henry's daughter, Queen Elizabeth, was responsible for producing two medals to celebrate the victory of the Spanish Armada in July 1588. These were known as the Bay Tree and Ark in Flood Medals, from their designs, and had a small suspension ring for wearing, usually around the neck. The medals were struck in gold, silver and copper, and are rare. The next British medal to appear was the Welch Medal, presented by King Charles I to Sir Robert Welch for gallantry at Edge Hill in 1642, during the Civil War. The first medal intended to be issued to all ranks in the Army—but it is doubtful whether all ranks did receive it—was the Dunbar Medal (Figs.2 and 3). It was issued following the Parliamentarians' victory over the Scots at Dunbar in 1650. This medal set a precedent which was not followed up until the granting of the Waterloo Medal in 1815. Cromwell also gave Commonwealth Naval Medals to officers engaged against the Dutch in the naval engagements of the 1650s.

King Charles II, William and Mary, and Queen Anne continued the tradition of issuing Naval Medals, and a number of very fine pieces were struck. King George I was responsible for re-instituting the Order of the Bath in 1725, while his son George II ordered a medal to be given to senior officers who fought at Culloden in April 1746 against Prince Charles Edward Stuart in the last battle to be fought on British soil. The medal, struck in gold with a loop for the ribbon, shows the Duke of Cumberland on the obverse, with the god Apollo and a slain dragon on the reverse. This medal was the first to be issued with a standard coloured ribbon, crimson with green borders. It has been disputed that this was ever an official issue, but is a most interesting and historical item.

Increasing numbers of medals were issued in the early years of King George III's reign, but these are usually rare as very few were granted. Examples are the Louisbourg (1758); Carib War (1773); Defence of Gibraltar (1782), and Isle of St. Vincent (1795). Following the British colonial expansion into India in the eighteenth century, the Honourable East India Company issued medals to their native troops. These unnamed medals continued to be large silver medallions suspended from the recipient's neck by a yellow cord. The East India Company medals are really the first of the early issues to come within financial reach of the average collector. Medals issued by the Company include the Deccan Medal (1784); Mysore Campaign (1792); Capture of Ceylon (1796); Seringapatam (1799), and Java (1811). The last two medals were also granted to European troops serving with the Company's forces.

The British Government struck Naval Gold Medals in 1795, following the commencement of the Napoleonic Wars in 1793. These very attractive and rare medals show a small figure of Victory standing on the prow of a Roman galley, crowning Britannia with a laurel wreath. They were originally awarded to Admirals and Captains of Lord Howe's fleet after the victory over the French off Ushant in June 1794, and were later also given

Fig. 1   Roman 'Phalera' (Breast Plate Medallion), c. A.D. 250

Fig. 2   (left) Obverse of Dunbar Medal 1650 (Cromwell)
Fig. 3   (right) Reverse of Dunbar Medal (House of Commons)

for the Nile, Trafalgar and other naval actions. There was still no provision, however, for the issue of medals to junior officers, petty officers and seamen. An attempt was made to rectify this by Alexander Davison, Lord Nelson's Prize Agent, who was responsible for selling vessels and their cargoes captured by Nelson's ships. Davison had medallions struck in gold, silver, bronze gilt and bronze, these being presented to all crew members and highly prized. The medals were not named, but privately named examples are occasionally found. The first was given for the Nile (1798) (Fig.4), followed by another in pewter for Trafalgar (1805). A Birmingham manufacturer, Matthew Boulton, also issued a pewter medal for Trafalgar. These unofficial medals were usually worn around the neck, suspended from a dark blue ribbon.

There were still no medals for the Army, however, except for those soldiers who had served in the Honourable East India Company's Army in India and who had received the Company's medals, as previously mentioned. This did not apply to senior officers, who were rewarded for the Battle of Maida (1806) by a Gold Medal, and for services in the Spanish Peninsular War (1808-14) and other theatres of war by Army Gold Medals and the Peninsular Gold Cross. The Army Gold Medals, issued in two sizes, show the seated figure of Britannia on the obverse with palm branch and shield, the reverse having the name of the battle for which the medal was

Fig. 4   Davison's Nile Medal, 1798

Fig. 5   Waterloo, 1815

5

awarded. Subsequent actions (up to two) were denoted by heavy gold bars attached to the ribbon. The recipient's name was engraved on the edge. Issue numbers were 85 Large (for General officers) and 599 Small (field officers). After the fourth action, the Peninsular Gold Cross was awarded, one of the most beautiful medals ever struck (*shown in colour on the cover*). This has the officer's first four battles shown on each arm, while subsequent actions are again indicated by gold bars. The recipient's name is again engraved around the edge. Only 163 Crosses were issued, the Duke of Wellington's Cross having nine bars. Both the Medals and Cross have a wide crimson ribbon with dark blue edges.

The first Army campaign medal issued to all ranks was the Waterloo Medal instituted in 1816 (Fig.5). This medal, bearing the Prince Regent's head on the obverse, and the seated winged figure of Victory on the reverse, was granted to all who took part in the battles of Ligny and Quatre Bras (16 June) and Waterloo (18 June). The medal was also given to the next-of-kin of men killed in these battles. The recipient's name and regiment were machine impressed around the edge, a steel clip and ring being used to attach the broad crimson blue-edged ribbon to the medal.

The striking of the Waterloo Medal was a unique event and no further campaign medals were struck during the reigns of George IV (1820-30) and William IV (1830-37), except for the East India Company's Burma Medal in 1826. King William did, however, establish the Long Service and Good Conduct Medal for the Royal Navy and Marines in 1831, for 21 years' service, and a similar medal for the Army in 1833, covering 21 years' service in the Infantry and 20 years in the Cavalry. A gratuity was also paid with these medals.

Although the Waterloo soldiers had been honoured in 1816, no campaign medals had been struck for the veterans of the Peninsular War (1808-14), the Mahratta and other Indian Wars (1803-26), and the Naval survivors of Nelson's epic sea victories over the French Navy. This unsatisfactory state of affairs continued after the death of George III in 1820 and was not settled until 1848, when Queen Victoria had been on the throne for eleven years. Several campaign medals had been issued during the early years of Victoria's reign and this added impetus to the demand that the earlier wars be recognised by the issue of medals. A petition was placed before the House of Lords in 1845 by the Duke of Richmond and, eventually, notices were issued at Horse Guards

Fig. 6   Military General Service 1793-1814

and the Admiralty on 1 June 1847, stating that all survivors from the Napoleonic Wars, 1793-1814, could apply for a medal provided they had proof of service. The Army medal, known as the Military General Service Medal (Fig.6), has as obverse the diademed 'young head' of Queen Victoria; the reverse depicts the Queen crowning the kneeling Duke of Wellington with a laurel wreath, the legend 'To The British Army' appearing around the top. The medals are named around the edge in roman capitals, the crimson blue-bordered ribbon being attached to the medal by means of a straight suspender. Twenty-nine bars were issued with the medal, fifteen being the maximum any one man could receive. These battle bars commemorate some of the bloodiest battles of the Peninsular War, such as Albuhera and Badajoz. Campaigns outside Europe were commemorated by bars such as Martinique (1809) and Fort Detroit (North America, 1812). Some of these bars are rare, especially as single issues.

The Naval equivalent of the Army medal was the Naval General Service Medal, (1793-1840), which was used for Naval actions up to Syria (1840). The obverse is the same as the Military Medal and the attractive reverse shows Britannia riding a sea horse (Fig.7). The recipient's name and rank (officers and warrant officers only), are impressed around the edge, but the ship's name is never shown. This can be checked on the Medal Rolls. Two hundred and thirty-one bars were sanctioned, with a maximum of seven to any one individual. Apart from commemorating such famous actions as Camperdown, the Nile, Copenhagen and Trafalgar, bars were granted for ship-to-ship battles, such as 'Surprise with Hermione' (October 1799), and 'Boat Service' actions. The bars for these are inscribed, e.g. '27th June 1803' (for capture of the French brig *Venteux* by two ship's boats from H.M.S. *Loire*). They are rare, as few men were engaged in these hand-to-hand actions. The medal has a distinctive white ribbon with blue edges.

Fig. 7   Naval General Service, 1793-1840

The early Indian veterans were rewarded in 1851 by the Army of India Medal, 1799-1826. This has the same obverse as the two previous medals, without the date, the reverse depicting a seated figure of Victory in front of a palm tree, with 'To the Army of India' around the top of the reverse. Named to British troops in roman capitals, and to Indians in script, the medal has an ornate suspender for the light blue ribbon. Twenty bars were struck for the medal, seven being the maximum, issued to Drummer Colston, 2/15th Bengal Native Infantry. The actions cover the period 1803 (Allighur) to 1826 (Bhurtpoor). These medals have always been scarce, especially to Europeans.

Queen Victoria

The long reign of Queen Victoria (sixty-four years, from 1837 to 1901) saw the issue of a large number of Campaign Medals, and also the introduction of Decorations for all ranks of the Army and Navy. These were sanctioned and issued by the British Government, except for the early Indian campaign medals, which were granted by the Governor-General's Office in India on behalf of Her Majesty. This practice continued up to the Indian Mutiny in 1857. Nearly all the medals issued in the early and middle years of Victoria's reign bear the 'young head' with 'Victoria Regina' legend, designed by W. Wyon, as used on the Military and Naval General Service Medals mentioned earlier. The bust of the Queen altered as she became older during her long reign, the final design appearing on the China 1900 Medal. The medals were usually struck in silver, except for a few of the later types, struck in bronze for native troops only.

The campaign medals and decorations issued during the reign were briefly as follows: Ghuznee Forts 1839, given on behalf of Shah Sujah in Afghanistan; Candahar, Ghuznee and Cabul 1841-42, with the Jellalabad Medal (two types) and Defence of Kelat-i-Ghilzie. All these were for the Afghan War 1841-42, Jellalabad medals to the 13th (Somerset Light) Infantry being highly prized. The next medal was for China 1842, this type being re-issued for the

1857-60 China War. The campaigns in the Scinde District of India (1843) produced another three medals and those to the 22nd Foot (Cheshires) are in demand. The Gwalior Campaign (1843) saw the issue of two bronze stars for 'Maharajpoor' (Fig.8) and 'Punniar', struck from metal taken from captured enemy cannon.

Meanwhile small native wars in the Eastern Cape Province of South Africa against the Kaffir tribes had been keeping the troops posted there very busy. These occurred in 1834-35, 1846-47 and 1850-53. The South Africa Medal 1853 was struck to cover all these campaigns. New Zealand also had a number of armed encounters between the settlers and the Maori tribes; the New Zealand Medal was given for these, with no less than twenty-nine different dated reverses (Fig.9), plus an undated type. Some of these dated reverses are rare, for example, '1846-65' given only to one recipient, Colonel R. H. McGregor, 65th (York and Lancaster) Regiment. The unofficial New Zealand Cross was given for the later Wars, this rare award for bravery (only 23 issued) was soon discontinued as it did not have official Government sanction.

Trouble again flared up in India in the 1840s with the Sikh Wars, 1845-46 and 1848-49. The Sutlej Medal was given for the first of these: the medal has the recipient's first battle shown on the reverse, with subsequent engagements indicated by bars, up to a maximum of three. Three-bar medals to the 31st (East Surrey) and 50th (Royal West Kent) Regiments are scarce. The Punjab Medal covered the second war and medals to the 24th Foot (2nd Warwickshires) with single 'Chilianwala' bar are worth having as the

Fig. 8   Gwalior Star, 'Maharajpoor' type, 1843

Fig. 9   New Zealand Medal
(reverse), 1860-66

8

Regiment suffered 524 casualties in this battle.

The India General Service Medal 1854-95 was instituted to cover all the small Indian wars on the North West and North East Frontiers of the country, also Persia, Burma (four Campaigns) and Malaya (Perak). Twenty-three bars were issued with the medal during its forty-one-year existence and some of them are rare. The maximum number of bars to one recipient was seven, and the medal was also struck in bronze for native followers.

The Crimean War 1854-55 was the first large war in Queen Victoria's reign, and is well remembered for the dreadful sufferings of the troops during the Russian winter. The heroic actions of the soldiers and sailors at the Alma, Balaklava (including the Charge of the Light Brigade), Inkermann and Sebastopol are commemorated by bars on the Crimea Medal (Fig.10). Recipients of this medal also received the Turkish Crimea Medal from the grateful Sultan of Turkey. The Royal Navy's actions in North Russian waters, where they bombarded the Forts of Sveaborg and Bomarsund, were recognised by the Baltic Medal 1854-55. The Victoria Cross was also first issued during the Crimea War to reward the bravery of soldiers and sailors of all ranks. Instituted in January 1856, the first award was won by Mate C. Lucas for bravery during the attack on Bomarsund in the Baltic, June 1854. A total of 111

Fig. 10   Crimea, 1854-55

Fig. 11   Victoria Cross

Fig. 12   Indian Mutiny, 1857-58

Fig. 13   Abyssinia, 1867-68

V.C.s were given during the war. A Victoria Cross is illustrated in Fig. 11. The Distinguished Conduct Medal was another medal for bravery which appeared during the Crimean War, by Royal Warrant dated December 1854. This medal was given to N.C.O.s and men for acts of bravery which did not warrant the award of the Victoria Cross. A similar medal, the Conspicuous Gallantry Medal, was given to seamen and Petty Officers in the Royal Navy. The latter decoration is rare, only 10 being awarded between 1854 and 1856.

Following the Crimean War, the Indian Mutiny flared up in 1857. The Indian Mutiny Medal 1857-58 struck for this war (Fig.12) commemorates the famous Defence and Relief of Lucknow, medals with 'Defence of Lucknow' bars to

original defenders from the 32nd (Duke of Cornwall's) Light Infantry always realising a good price. The 'Delhi' bar on this medal covers the siege of that town, the recapture of which played a vital part in the final British victory.

The Fenian troubles in Canada during the 1860s were responsible for the issue of the Canada General Service Medal 1866-70. This covered the Fenian Raids into the country between the dates stated, also Sir Garnet Wolseley's Red River expedition of 1870. The British Government did not originally intend to issue a medal for these minor wars and the medal only appeared in 1899. Medals to British troops, especially with

Fig. 14   Ashantee, 1873-74

Fig. 15   South Africa, 1877-79

'Red River 1870' bar, are very scarce. The Abyssinian War 1867–68 saw the issue of a unique medal in size (smaller than usual) and design (Fig 13). The British recipients' names were embossed on the reverse, a very expensive process and not attempted again. Medals to the 100 members of the Royal Naval Rocket Brigade are much sought after.

The Ashantee War Medal 1873-74 has an unusual reverse, depicting a 'bush fight' between British troops and natives (Fig.14). One bar, 'Coomassie', was given to those who captured King Coffee Kalikali's capital. The Zulu War 1879 and South African native wars against the Gaika and Galeka tribes of the Eastern Cape were responsible for the re-issue of the South Africa 1853 Medal without the date and with 'dated' bars, e.g. '1877-8-9' (Fig.15). Medals to members

of the 1/24th Foot (Warwickshires), massacred at Isandhlwana, and to the heroic defenders of Rorke's Drift (2/24th Foot) are keenly sought by collectors. A complete Medal Roll containing all the known names of those who took part in the 1877-79 campaigns has been published, and will stimulate even greater interest in this well-documented series of native wars. The Afghan War Medal 1878-80 (Fig.16) with its large square bars is of great interest, as again a good deal of information is available on this war. Medals with 'Kandahar' bar often have the bronze Kabul to Kandahar Star 1880 with them, this being given to those who took part in Lord Roberts's epic 300-mile march to relieve that city. Medals to the 66th (Royal Berkshires), who were killed fighting bravely to the end at Maiwand, are valued items.

Fig. 16   Afghanistan, 1878-80

Fig. 17   Egypt, 1882-89

Egypt was the next scene of action, the distinctive 'Sphinx' reverse medals (Fig.17) being given for the 1882 and 1884-89 (Sudan) campaigns, the latter including the failed attempt to relieve General Gordon in Khartoum. Some famous battles were fought in the Sudan against the Mahdi's fanatical followers, these including actions at El Teb, Tamaai and Abu Klea, for which bars were awarded. Thirteen bars in all were given with the medals, with a maximum of seven to one man, Captain J. R. D. Beech. Five-bar medals are rare and four-bar items are not common. The large Khedive's Bronze Stars (Fig.18) usually accompany the Egypt Medals.

The North-West Canada Medal 1885 with scarce 'Saskatchewan' bar appeared next for

Riel's Rebellion, only local troops being used in this campaign. More trouble in the Cape Province of South Africa saw the issue of the Cape of Good Hope General Service Medal 1880-97 with three bars; again local troops only were involved. Three-bar medals (13 only given) are rare. A bronze star, the Ashantee Star 1896, was struck to cover another small campaign in this West African territory, followed by the East and West Africa Medal 1887-1900, for small African wars. This medal is a re-issue of the Ashantee Medal 1873-74, with twenty-three bars being given with the medal during the thirteen years in which it was current. The Central Africa Medal 1891-98, same striking as the previous medal but with a different ribbon, and the East and Central

Fig. 18   Khedive's Star, 1882 type

Fig. 19   British South Africa
Company's Medal, 1890-96
(reverse). 'Matabeleland' 1893

Africa Medal 1897-99 were also issued during this period, illustrating the British interest in Africa during the late nineteenth century. The latter two medals are very scarce. Chartered Companies in Africa gave medals to the Queen's forces as well, native troops being mostly involved together with local white settlers. Examples are the Royal Niger Company's Medal 1886-97 and the British South Africa Company's Medal 1890-97, the latter for the Mashona and Matabele Wars in Rhodesia (Fig.19). This practice was also followed by the British North Borneo Company in the Far East, who issued Company Medals between 1897 and 1916, followed by a General Service Medal in 1937.

The British Government decided in the 1890s to give another General Service Medal, the India 1895 Medal, to replace the then-existing 1854 Medal (Fig.20) as this type had been in existence for over forty years. Six bars were issued with the new medal up until the Queen's death in January 1901. The rarest of these is the 'Defence of Chitral 1895' bar. The medal was again used at the beginning of King Edward VII's reign with 'Waziristan 1901-02' bar, the date '1895' being removed from the reverse of the medal.

The reconquest of the Sudan in 1896 led to the striking of the Queen's Sudan Medal 1896-97 (Fig.21). No bars were given with the medal, examples of which to the 21st Lancers are very desirable. The medal ribbon is said to represent the desert (yellow), the Khalifa's army (black), divided by a thin red stripe representing the British forces.

The last big conflict in the Queen's reign was the South African War, 1899-1902, for which the Queen's South Africa Medal was issued. This medal (Fig.22) has always been popular with medal collectors and, apart from three very scarce bars, is still reasonably priced. The three scarce bars are 'Defence of Mafeking', 'Relief of Mafeking' and 'Wepener'. Twenty-six bars were given with the medal, which was also awarded without a bar, with a maximum of nine to one man (Army) or eight (Navy). Battle bars are found commemorating several famous engagements in the early part of the war, e.g. 'Talana' and 'Elandslaagte', together with those given for the Defence and Relief of Mafeking, Kimberley and Ladysmith. Five 'State' bars were also awarded, 'Cape Colony', 'Natal', 'Rhodesia' (scarce), 'Orange Free State' and 'Transvaal' for small actions not covered by the 'battle' bars. The Queen's Medal was first struck with the raised dates '1899-1900' on the reverse, but these were soon erased from the dies, as the war continued until 1902. The raised-date reverse medals are rare as only one complete unit, Lord Strathcona's Horse, was issued with them. The medals continued to be struck with the dates erased until a new reverse die could be made. The difference can be detected quite easily as the wreath in Britannia's right hand points to the 'R' in 'Africa' on the first type, and to the 'F' in the second. There are a number of good books

Fig. 20   India General Service,
1854

Fig. 21   Queen's Sudan Medal,
1896-97

available on the war and a large and interesting collection can be made of medals issued during this period, as many different Imperial regiments and local units were involved. The Mayor of Kimberley issued an unofficial Star and a Medal (rare) to the defenders of that town. Another very scarce medal, struck in silver and bronze, was given to the defenders of the copper town of O'okiep in Namaqualand by the Cape Copper Company.

A variety of the Queen's Medal, The Queen's Mediterranean Medal, was given to troops who manned garrisons in that area during the South African War. These are very scarce. Another medal which should also be represented in a South African War collection is the Anglo-Boer War Medal, issued in 1920 to all ranks of the Boer forces who served against the British between 1899 and 1902.

The Chinese Boxer Rebellion also occurred during 1900 and was commemorated by another issue of the earlier China Medal 1857-60, with the last bust of Queen Victoria on the obverse. Three bars were issued with the China 1900 Medal, the rarest of these being for the 'Defence of Legations' in Peking (Fig.23). Medals to the Royal Welch Fusiliers with 'Relief of Pekin' bar are always of interest to collectors, as this was the only British regiment present as a unit.

Mention must also be made of three important decorations issued during the later years of Queen Victoria's reign. These were the Albert Medals in Gold (First Class) and Bronze (Second Class), for saving life at sea (blue and white ribbon), and for saving life on land (red and white

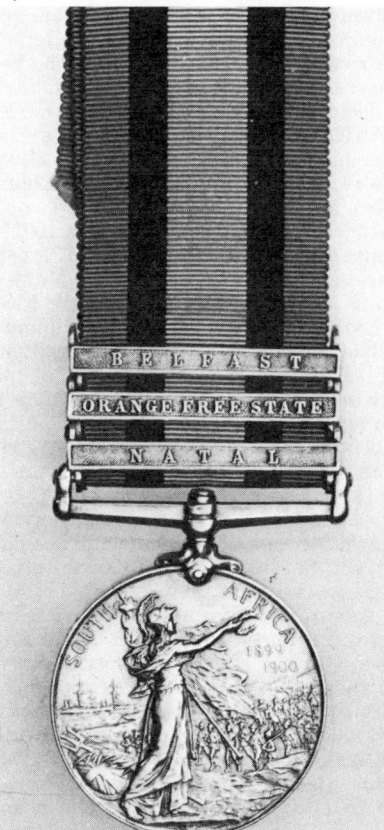

Fig. 22   Queen's South Africa
Medal, 1899-1902 (reverse), with
rare 'raised dates'

Fig. 23   China, 1900, with rare
'Defence of Legations' bar

ribbon). These handsome oval decorations (Fig. 24) were established by the Queen in 1866 and 1877 and are rare. The George Cross and George Medal, instituted in 1940, superseded these Medals, it being decided in 1949 that the Bronze Medal only should still be awarded posthumously after this date.

The Royal Red Cross was instituted by the Queen in 1883, as a Military decoration for ladies only. There are two Classes, the First Class (R.R.C.) in gold, and the Second Class (A.R.R.C.), both of these being awarded to all ranks of the Nursing Services. This decoration covers devoted work by nurses in wartime with the Army, in Naval and Military Hospitals, and in Hospital Ships.

The Distinguished Service Order appeared in 1886 and was intended to reward individual acts of bravery or distinguished service by officers in wartime. An interesting aspect of the award is that the recipient has to be previously mentioned in dispatches for services in the field. The early

Fig. 24   Albert Medal in gold (1st Class)

Crosses, awarded before 1890, were made of gold and these are rare; since then they have been made of silver-gilt. This very attractive decoration has always been highly prized by collectors, and gallantry groups of medals containing the D.S.O. are in demand.

King Edward VII and King George V

King Edward ascended the British throne in 1901 at the age of 59, and died nine years later. The South African War was still on when he became king, guerrilla warfare continuing until May 1902. It was decided, therefore, to strike the King's South Africa Medal, with the King's bust in Field Marshal's uniform on the obverse, and using the same second-type reverse as had appeared on the Queen's South Africa Medal. Two bars, 'South Africa 1901' and 'South Africa 1902' were always given with the medal (Fig.25), except for a few rare no-bar medals awarded to Nurses. An interesting point concerning the King's Medal is that it could only be given to a recipient who already had the Queen's Medal, and could not be awarded separately. Those who did not qualify for the King's Medal, the qualifying time being eighteen months counted backwards from 1 June 1902, received one or both of the 'dated' bars on the Queen's Medal, provided that they were in the country in 1901 or 1902.

A very attractive award, the Transport Medal (Fig.26), was given to officers of ships which took troops out to South Africa and China during the campaigns in those countries. This portrays the King in Admiral's uniform, the reverse featuring a map of the Atlantic and Indian Ocean areas of the globe, with the H.M. Transport *Ophir* superimposed thereon. Two bars, 'S.Africa 1899-1902' and 'China 1900' were given with the medal, two-bar medals being very scarce. Another Ashanti War had also broken out in 1900; the medal for this campaign was sanctioned in October 1901, so therefore this issue bears the King's head. The Ashanti 1900 is very scarce, especially to Europeans, as most British troops were engaged in South Africa at the time. Only one bar was given, 'Kumassi'.

An additional African medal, the Africa General Service Medal, appeared in 1902, to replace the East and West Africa Medal 1887-1900. This medal has the same Britannia and lion reverse as the earlier East and Central Africa Medal 1897-99, with the word 'Africa' appearing in the exergue. Thirty-four bars were issued with the King Edward obverse, a very large number for such a short period, including fifteen for Northern and Southern Nigeria alone, the remainder being for small actions in East and West Africa and Somaliland. The medal was used again during King George V's reign with another ten bars and these are all extremely scarce.

The next small war to break out during King Edward's reign occurred in the remote mountain kingdom of Tibet in 1903. Following a boundary dispute, a column of Indian troops with a small British force (mainly from the 1st Battalion of the Royal Fusiliers) entered the country under Colonel Younghusband. The Tibet Medal 1903-4, with one bar 'Gyantse', was issued to cover this expedition. The medal has a fine reverse showing the Tibetan fortress of Potala Lhassa. This campaign was followed by the Natal Rebellion in 1906 among the Zulu people in South Africa over hut taxes. The Natal 1906 Medal, with one bar '1906', is interesting in that a 'coinage' type head of the King was used. The very attractive reverse illustrates Britannia supporting a female figure representing Natal (Fig.27). Only local troops were used during the uprising.

Fig. 25   King's South Africa
Medal, 1901-02

Fig. 26   Transport Medal,
1899-1902, rare two-bar type

It was decided to strike a new Indian General Service Medal during King Edward's reign, this medal being used between 1908 and 1935, thus including the reign of King George V when the bust of King George was used. The reverse shows the Jamrud Fort in the Khyber Pass, this reverse remaining unchanged during the medal's existence. One bar, 'North West Frontier 1908', was given in King Edward's reign, and eleven during that of King George V, the latter including the rare 'Waziristan 1925' bar issued only to the Royal Air Force.

Decorations issued between 1901 and 1910 were the same types as previously awarded in Queen Victoria's reign, except for changes in the Royal cypher on the Distinguished Service Order from 'V.R.I.' to 'E.VII.R'. The Distinguished Conduct

Medal now had the King's bust in Field Marshal's uniform on the obverse instead of the Victorian trophy of arms, the practice of showing the Sovereign's head on this medal continuing from this time onwards. Conspicuous Gallantry Medals from this period, again showing the King's bust but in Admiral's uniform, are rare, only two awards being made, both in 1904. A new Naval gallantry decoration for officers, the Conspicuous Service Cross, was instituted in June 1901; these are also rare, only eight being awarded up to 1914. This decoration became the Distinguished Service Cross in 1914 with the 'GRI' (King George V) cypher. The Edward Medal was established in 1907 to reward gallant acts carried out by miners and quarrymen. These rare medals were given in two classes, silver and bronze, and were later replaced by the George Cross and George Medal in 1940. It was decided in 1949 to issue the bronze medal in future only as a posthumous award. The King's Police Medal appeared in 1909, to be given to Police and Fire Brigade officers for gallant and distinguished service.

King George V came to the throne in 1910, and reigned for twenty-six years. This reign saw the end of the Edwardian era in the tremendous conflict of the Great War 1914-18. The first medal issued during the new King's reign was the Naval General Service Medal, for minor naval operations, which was authorised in 1915, the first bar with the medal being 'Persian Gulf 1909-1914'. Medals with this bar are the only examples of the type which show the recipient's ship. The medal was again used during the reigns of King George VI and Queen Elizabeth II, until 1964. Only two more bars were given with the King George V issue, 'Iraq 1919-20' and 'N.W. Persia 1920', both rare.

The Great War began, for Great Britain, on 4 August 1914, British troops being landed in France shortly afterwards. The British Expeditionary Force came into action almost immediately, being heavily involved in the early actions, including the retreat from Mons and the first Battle of Ypres. The 1914 Star (often called the 'Mons' Star) was issued in 1917 to cover the early battles in France and Flanders, with a sew-on bar, '5th Aug - 22nd Nov 1914', later given to those who were actually under fire during this period. This Star (Fig.28) was given only to those who served in France and Belgium, so that others who were engaged in the War during this period but served in other theatres, e.g. the Royal Navy in the Falklands, received the 1914-15 Star. This award is identical to the 1914 type, including the

Fig. 27   Natal, 1906

18

Fig. 28   1914 Star

France in 1918, which the Allies barely managed to contain. The tide, however, had slowly started to turn against the Central Powers, and 1918 saw the final collapse of Turkey and Austria, followed by the final Armistice with Germany on 11 November. No special stars or medals were issued to those who took part in the last three years of the War, the British War Medal being instituted in 1919 for all those who served between 1914 and 1918, later extended to 1920 to cover service in North and South Russia. This medal, with its orange-centred white, black and blue striped ribbon, is one of the most familiar awards issued. No bars were given with the medal because of the number of battles involved and the inevitable cost. About six and a half million British War medals were given in silver, with about 100,000 in bronze to native Labour Corps members; these latter are fairly scarce. The bronze Victory Medal, with its attractive rainbow-coloured ribbon, is usually seen with the British War Medal, and a large and still very reasonable collection can be made of these medals as so many different regiments and units were involved in the War. The Victory Medal is sometimes found with a small oak leaf attached to the ribbon, indicating a Mention in Dispatches. Only one oak leaf could be worn regardless of the number of Mentions.

Recipients of either the 1914 or 1914-15 Stars (a man could only receive one of these and never both), were automatically entitled to both the British War and Victory Medals and therefore these Stars should always be collected in trios with the medals. An interesting collection can, however, be made up from single Stars, separated from the other two medals, especially of the 1914 type. Some regiments that were entitled to this Star are very scarce, e.g. the Royal Flying Corps, the Royal Naval Air Service, the Royal Navy (these were given to Naval personnel who served ashore at Antwerp in 1914), and units who took part in the first battles of the war. Stars and medals to officers are always of interest, the rank and regiment being shown on the Stars, but only the rank and name on the Medals, except for Royal Artillery and Royal Air Force officer recipients. A very useful book to have is *Officers Died in the Great War 1914-19*, reprinted by J. L. R. Samson in 1975, giving details of all officers who were killed or died in the war.

The Mercantile Marine War Medal 1914-18 in bronze, with its distinctive red and green ribbon with narrow white centre stripe (these colours are said to represent a ship's mast and navigating

red, white and blue ribbon, except that the centre scroll has the dates '1914-15' instead of '1914'. No bar was given with the 1914-15 Star, which represents service in the 1915 battles on the Western Front in France and Belgium, when gas was first used, the Gallipoli landings, the war against the Turks in Mesopotamia, and the campaigns against the Germans in South West and East Africa. The war dragged on through 1916, with the terrible Somme battles, the Naval Battle of Jutland, and continuing campaigns in Meso-potamia, Palestine and East Africa. The year 1917 saw little progress in the Ypres Salient, the Battle of Messines Ridge, the dreadful carnage in the mud at Passchendaele, a year marked also by the collapse of the Russian monarchy and the entry of the United States of America into the war. The Germans launched a tremendous offensive in lights), was given to all who served in the Mercantile Marine from 1914 to 1918. This medal is usually seen with the British War Medal only and not the Victory Medal. Another fairly scarce medal is the Territorial Force War Medal 1914-19, the ribbon for this bronze medal being golden-yellow with two green stripes. The medal was given to all members of the Territorial Force who had completed 4 years' service prior to August 1914 and who had rejoined before 30 September 1914. Recipients of the medal had also to be ineligible for either the 1914 or 1914-15 Stars. This makes the medal scarce, as most of those serving in 1914 and 1915 had served in a theatre of war and were thus entitled to the Stars. The Territorial Medal is usually found with the British War and Victory Medals, being worn after these.

Although the existing Gallantry Decorations continued into the reign of King George V, it was found that there were not sufficient grades of these to reward the large number of brave acts performed during the Great War. The British Government therefore decided to supplement the existing decorations in 1914, commencing with the Military Cross for junior Army officers (up to the rank of Captain), this being instituted on 28 December 1914. The equivalent decoration for the Royal Navy, the Conspicuous Service Cross, had previously been converted to the Distinguished Service Cross in October 1914. At the same time another medal, the Distinguished Service Medal, was introduced as a similar award to Petty Officers and seamen in the Royal Navy. Non-commissioned officers and other ranks in the Army, however, had to wait longer for their award to appear, as the Military Medal was not instituted until March 1916. All these awards were also given to members of the Royal Flying Corps and Royal Naval Air Service until the formation of the Royal Air Force in April 1918, which united these two Services. It should be noted here that officers' decorations are not officially named, although privately named examples are sometimes found. Decorations to N.C.O.s and other ranks are always officially named around the edge of the medal.

Following the formation of the Royal Air Force in 1918, it was decided to give the new Service its own decorations, so the Distinguished Flying Cross (for officers) and the Distinguished Flying Medal (for N.C.O.s and other ranks) were instituted in June 1918, to reward acts of gallantry performed while flying in operations against the enemy. The Air Force Cross and Air Force Medal also appeared at the same time, to recognise brave deeds in the air, but not against an enemy and in peace time. These attractive decorations have their own distinctive ribbons, diagonal violet and white stripes (for the D.F.C.) and diagonal red and white stripes (for the A.F.C.). The D.F.M. and A.F.M. have the same colours with narrower stripes. The stripes were originally horizontal in all cases, this being altered to the diagonal type in July 1919. Some of the early decorations awarded prior to 1919 are found with the old horizontal-striped ribbons. Royal Air Force personnel are, of course, entitled to receive the Victoria Cross and the Distinguished Service Order. An interesting point concerning the Victoria Cross is that up to 1918 this award had a crimson ribbon for Army recipients and a dark blue ribbon for the Navy. This was altered to

Fig. 29   General Service, 1918-64

crimson for all recipients following the establishment of the Royal Air Force in April 1918. It should also be noted that decorations are invariably accompanied by at least one Campaign or Service medal, single items awarded for military gallantry which appear on the market from time to time having usually lost their accompanying service medal or medals.

A General Service Medal for the Army and Royal Air Force, the equivalent of the 1915 Naval General Service Medal, was issued in 1918 (Fig. 29). The first type has the 'coinage' head of King George V; five bars were given with this medal, the scarcest being 'Southern Desert: Iraq', only awarded to four squadrons of the Royal Air Force. The second type has the crowned head of King George V with 'Northern Kurdistan' bar and this is rare, being given only to the Iraq Levies and three R.A.F. squadrons. The medal, with different Sovereign's busts but the same reverse, was again used during the reigns of King George VI and Queen Elizabeth II up to 1964.

King George VI and Queen Elizabeth II

King George VI became King in 1937 following the abdication of his brother, King Edward VIII. Only one new medal, bearing the crowned head of King George VI, was issued before the outbreak of war in 1939, this being the India General Service Medal 1936–39. Two bars were given with this short-lived type, 'North West Frontier 1936-37' and 'North West Frontier 1937-39', medals to British troops being quite scarce. The medal was abolished after the war, following the independence of India in 1947.

The Second World War began in September 1939 and ended in May 1945 (the war in Europe) and August 1945 (war against Japan). This tremendous conflict was commemorated by the issue of six campaign stars and two medals by the British Government. These were the 1939-45 Star with dark blue, red and light blue striped ribbon (to indicate the Royal Navy, Army and Royal Air Force); the Atlantic Star for the Battle of the Atlantic (the watered blue, white and green ribbon representing the Atlantic Ocean); and the scarce Air Crew Europe Star (for flying operations

Fig. 30 Air Crew Europe Star, 1939-44

between September 1939 and June 1944) (Fig.30). The pale blue ribbon with this Star illustrates the R.A.F. colour, the narrow black and yellow edges indicating day and night operations over Europe. The Africa Star (June 1940-May 1943) has a pale beige-coloured ribbon for the sands of the Western Desert, with a central red stripe and narrow dark blue and light blue stripes, again representing the three Services. The Pacific Star and Burma Star (1941-45) were given for the campaigns in the Far East. The Italy Star (1943-45) ribbon represents the colours of that country's flag, as does the ribbon of the France and Germany Star (1944-45) in red, white and blue for the national colours of France and the Netherlands. The 1939-45 Star has one bar, 'Battle of Britain', given to fighter pilots only who took part in that battle. The Africa Star is sometimes found with one of the following bars. '1st Army', '8th Army' (to the Army) or 'North Africa 1942-43' (for the Royal Navy and R.A.F.). An arabic number '1' or '8' on the ribbon, when this is worn alone, indicates entitlement to the numbered bars, with a small silver rosette for the 'North Africa' bar. No bars were given with the Italy Star. Concerning the Atlantic Star (with France and Germany or Air Crew Europe bars), the Air Crew Europe Star (with France and Germany or Atlantic bars), and the France and Germany Star (Atlantic or Air Crew Europe bar), only one Star could be worn, plus one bar only, where a recipient qualified for a second of these three Stars. A silver rosette sewn on the ribbon, again when this was worn alone, indicates a bar. The Pacific Star has the 'Burma' bar, the Burma Star having the 'Pacific' bar, when the holder is entitled to both awards.

The Defence Medal (for service in areas subject to air attack) and the War Medal 1939-45 were given in addition to the Stars. The medals are struck in cupro-nickel except for the Canadian issues, which were struck in silver. Nearly all these World War II Stars and Medals were issued unnamed except for those given to Australian and South African recipients; these are found named in small capitals with serial number and name only. The larger Commonwealth countries also gave a separate Service Medal to their troops, the Canadian and South African types again being struck in silver.

The Naval General Service and General Service Medals continued during the King's reign, using the 'crowned head' obverse of King George VI (Fig.31). Six bars were issued with the Naval medal between 1937 and 1952, including the rare 'Yangtze 1949' type. The Army and R.A.F. medal King George VI type has five bars, including the rare 'Bomb and Mine Clearance' issues. The existing Gallantry Decorations continued to be awarded during this period, with altered cypher or bust, the George Cross and George Medal being added to these in 1940 to reward civilian bravery. Decorations given between 1939 and 1945 are much scarcer than those awarded for the Great War 1914-18, and are thus more expensive. A Mention in Dispatches was again indicated by a small bronze oak leaf, fixed to the War Medal ribbon.

The Korean War began in 1950 and was still continuing when Queen Elizabeth came to the throne in 1952. The Korean Medal (Fig.32) was issued in this year, with the 'uncrowned head' of the Queen, the medal being struck in cupro-

nickel. The Canadian version was struck in silver, with 'Canada' in the reverse exergue. The South African Government issued its own distinctive medal in silver; these are very scarce as only one squadron (No. 2) from the South African Air Force served in the war. The Korean Medal is usually seen in pair with the United Nations Korea Medal in bronze. Medals to the Gloucester Regiment are always popular among collectors.

The Africa General Service Medal, first issued in 1902 with King Edward VII's bust, and later that of King George V, appeared again in 1955 with the Queen's portrait and the 'Kenya' bar. The Naval General Service and General Service Medals were continued until 1964, the Naval medal having seven new bars, with the two rare 'Bomb and Mine Clearance' types. The Army and R.A.F. had five new bars, including the scarce 'Near East' bar. The Campaign Service Medal was struck in 1964, to be used by all the Services and replacing the former two General Service medals.

Fig. 31 Naval General Service, 1915-62

This has a plain reverse, with the words 'For Campaign Service' within a wreath and crown. Six bars have so far been issued (Fig.33), the rarest being 'South Vietnam', given to Australian and New Zealand troops serving in that area. A medal was also struck in 1968 for the Vietnam War, nearly all recipients again being from Australia and New Zealand. This medal often appears with the Vietnam Medal, given by the South Vietnamese Government.

The usual Gallantry Decorations have been continued in the Queen's reign. They are rare, as not many have been awarded and a large number of the recipients are still serving with the Armed Forces. The Queen's Gallantry Medal appeared in 1974, as an additional reward for exceptional acts of bravery by members of the Services and civilians. The Queen's Commendation for Brave Conduct is also seen occasionally: this is a silver oak leaf worn on the ribbon of the appropriate General Service Medal, or on the uniform if no campaign medal or bar was issued for the appropriate action.

Fig. 32   Korea, 1950-53

Fig. 33   Campaign Service, 1962 onwards

British Orders of Knighthood

The earliest of these is the Most Noble Order of the Garter, founded by King Edward III around 1348. The Order consists of the Sovereign and twenty-five Knights-Companion. The Most Ancient and Most Noble Order of the Thistle, founded in 1687 and revived in 1703, has only sixteen Knights of Scottish origin, making this another very scarce award. The Most Illustrious Order of St. Patrick was founded in 1783 and discontinued in 1922, following the establishment of the Irish Free State. The insignia of all these Orders are returnable following the death of the recipient, and so very rarely appear on the market. Privately made contemporary copies, some of these being heavily jewelled and enamelled, do, however, become available from time to time and these usually fetch high prices in auction. The letters distinguishing the three Orders are, respectively, K.G., K.T. and K.P.

The Most Honourable Order of the Bath is an important award, many famous military officers having been made members. Founded in 1725, it was subdivided into two divisions in 1815 by the Prince Regent (who later became King George IV), namely Military and Civil. The Military Order consists of three Classes, G.C.B. (Knights Grand Cross), K.C.B. (Knights Commander) and C.B. (Companions). The Civil Division, originally in one Class only, was increased to three Classes in 1847 to bring it into line with the Military Division. The Badges of the Order were made of gold up to 1887 and silver-gilt thereafter. Medal groups to officers containing the Order of the Bath are prized by collectors.

Mention must be made here of the Royal Guelphic Order, again instituted by the Prince Regent in 1815, to be given to British and Hanoverian subjects as a reward for outstanding military and civil services. The Order consisted of three Classes, no further awards being made to British subjects after Queen Victoria's accession to the throne in 1837. This rare award is occasionally seen with the Waterloo and/or the Naval or Military General Service Medals for the period 1793-1814, and is much sought after.

The Most Distinguished Order of St. Michael and St. George, founded in 1818 and originally for service in the Ionian Isles, was another award instituted by the Prince Regent. The Order consists of three Classes, G.C.M.G. (Knights or Dames Grand Cross), K. or D.C.M.G. (Knights or Dames Commander) and C.M.G. (Companions), being given to both men and women who have performed valuable services in the Colonies or Commonwealth countries. This award was again issued in gold up to 1887 and silver-gilt thereafter. Many distinguished members of the Services have this Order among their decorations and service medals. Until 1917 the C.B. and C.M.G. were both worn as breast badges with ornate gold buckles, mounted on the same ribbon bar as the recipient's other medals. This practice was discontinued in that year, following the introduction of the Order of the British Empire, when all three Orders were worn around the neck.

A rare Order instituted during British rule in India during the nineteenth century was the Most Exalted Order of the Star of India (1861), in three Classes, Knights Grand Commander (G.C.S.I.), Knights Commander (K.C.S.I.) and Companions (C.S.I.). Another scarce Indian award was the Most Eminent Order of the Indian Empire, founded in 1878, again in three Classes, Knights Grand Commander (G.C.I.E.), Knights Commander (K.C.I.E.) and Companions (C.I.E.). Both Orders were abolished following India's independence in 1947. Lower grades of these awards do sometimes appear in auction, usually with Indian General Service medals, from high-ranking former members of the Indian Army and Civil Service.

The Royal Victorian Order was founded by Queen Victoria in 1896, this honour being unusual in that it is given by the Sovereign for personal services to the Crown. There are five Classes, Knights or Dames Grand Cross (G.C.V.O.), Knights or Dames Commander (K. or D.C.V.O.), Commanders (C.V.O.), Members 4th Class and 5th Class (M.V.O.). There is also the Royal Victorian Medal, in silver-gilt, silver and bronze.

The most recent of the British Orders of Chivalry is the Most Excellent Order of the British Empire, with two Divisions, Civil and Military, instituted in 1917 in five Classes. These are Knights or Dames Grand Cross (G.B.E.), Knights or Dames Commander (K. or D.B.E.), Commanders (C.B.E.), Officers (O.B.E.) and Members (M.B.E.). The ribbon of the Order was originally purple, but this was altered in 1937 to rose-pink with pearl grey edges. At the same time the centre Britannia badge of the Order was changed to show the combined busts of King George V and Queen Mary (Fig.34). The same ribbon is used for Military awards of the Order,

Fig. 34   Breast Star, Knight Grand Cross, Order of the British Empire (G.B.E.)

with the addition of a narrow pearl grey stripe. Two associated gallantry medals, the British Empire Medal and the Empire Gallantry Medal, were instituted in 1917 and 1922. The 1917 Medal was superseded in 1922 by another British Empire Medal, of the same size and design as the Empire Gallantry type, in two Classes, Civil and Military, with 'For Meritorious Service' or 'For Gallantry' on the reverse. The medal ribbon has a small silver emblem representing two crossed oak leaves when the Medal is awarded for gallantry. The Empire Gallantry Medal was replaced by the George Cross in September 1940.

King Edward VII instituted a rare Order in 1902, this being the Order of Merit, again a personal award from the Sovereign. There is only one Class and membership is restricted to twenty-four recipients. It is given with swords (Military) and without (Civil). These rare awards seldom appear on the market.

A fairly recent addition to the British Orders of Knighthood is the Knights Bachelor Badge (Fig.35), founded in 1926 by King George V. This was originally a large oval gilt-enamel award, with a pin back so that it could be worn as a breast badge. It was later altered to a smaller type of Neck Badge, the ribbon being brick red with orange edges. A recent recipient of the Badge is the famous Sir Douglas Bader, World War II air ace.

Fig. 35 Knights Bachelor Badge (1st type)

Long Service and Miscellaneous

Another interesting area of medal collecting which is now coming into its own is the study of Long Service and Territorial medals. Long Service and Good Conduct Medals were first issued during the reign of King William IV (1830-37), commencing with the Army medal, instituted in July 1830. The Navy medal followed shortly afterwards in August 1831. The first Army issues show a trophy of arms on the obverse, containing a shield bearing the Hanoverian coat of arms, and the reverse has the inscription 'For Long Service and Good Conduct'. This design continued into Queen Victoria's reign, the Hanoverian coat of arms being replaced by the Royal coat of arms (Fig.36). This handsome-looking medal was awarded throughout the Queen's reign until 1902, the same obverse also being used for the Distinguished Conduct Medal during the period. The reverse lettering and ribbon suspender were altered in the later issues, and the medals are found named in impressed letters or engraved. The original qualification for the medal was

21 years' service in the Infantry, Artillery or Engineers, or 20 years in the Cavalry: it was later altered to 18 years' service for all arms of the Service. The soldier had in addition to have at least three Good Conduct badges.

A most interesting collection can be made of these Victorian issues, showing the 'numbered' Foot regiments up to 1881, followed by the 'county' regimental types as they became after that date. Medals to cavalry regiments are also very desirable. The practice of featuring the Sovereign's head on the obverse began with King Edward VII and is still observed today with the Queen Elizabeth II issues. Long Service Medals struck especially for the Colonies and Commonwealth countries are scarce, especially the early issues.

The Royal Navy version of the Long Service and Good Conduct Medal began as a slightly smaller

Fig. 36 Victorian Army Long Service and Good Conduct Medal

medal, with an anchor on the obverse, and these are extremely scarce. The early Victorian issues have the Queen's head on the obverse, with a $1\frac{1}{2}$ inch suspender for the ribbon, the reverse showing an old wooden line-of-battle ship (Fig.37). This reverse has continued to be used until the present day, the obverse changing with each successive Sovereign. Later Victorian issues have a narrower ($1\frac{1}{4}$ inch) ribbon suspender. The medals are found with engraved or impressed naming. Qualification for the award was originally 21 years of exemplary service, this being later reduced to 15 years. An interesting collection can again be made of these medals, showing all the early ranks of the recipients (most of these now abolished), and all the different ships' names.

The Royal Air Force have their own version of the Long Service and Good Conduct Medal, this award featuring an eagle on the reverse. Three types have so far been issued, with the heads of King George V, King George VI and Queen Elizabeth II.

The Meritorious Service Medal is another collectable item; it was instituted in 1845, Victorian issues being very scarce. The medal was originally issued with a gratuity and later, during the Great War 1914-18, given as a gallantry award for brave acts performed while not engaged against the enemy. Royal Naval issues awarded between 1919 and 1928 are well worth looking for; they can be identified by the King being in Admiral's uniform. Similar medals given to the Royal Flying Corps and Royal Air Force are likewise desirable. The British Empire Medal replaced the Royal Naval and Royal Air Force Meritorious Service Medals in 1928, but the Army medal has been retained up to the present day, only the Sovereign's head altering on the obverse for each successive reign. M.S.M.s to Colonial forces are very scarce and are sought after by collectors abroad.

Medals awarded to the Volunteer forces are increasing in popularity. They are the obsolete Volunteer Officers Decoration (Fig.38) and

Fig. 37 Victorian Naval Long Service and Good Conduct Medal

Fig. 38 Volunteer Officers Decoration (Victorian issue)

Fig. 39   Hungarian Order of Merit (Breast Badge)

Volunteer Long Service Medal, the latter usually named to a number of varied and unusual local units. The Militia and Imperial Yeomanry Long Service Medals (1904-08) are both very scarce items, these medals being easily distinguishable by their light blue and light yellow ribbons. The Efficiency Decoration (for officers) and Territorial Efficiency Medal (for N.C.O.s and other ranks), the latter award later becoming the Efficiency Medal, were the next to appear. The Royal Navy have their own special awards, including the Royal Naval Reserve Decoration (for officers) and the Royal Naval Reserve Long Service Medal (Petty Officers and seamen). The Royal Air Force equivalent is the Air Efficiency Award. There have been quite a number of varieties of Army Territorial and Royal Naval Volunteer medals issued during this century, including additional medals struck for the Colonies and Commonwealth countries, and a representative collection of all these types is most attractive.

Foreign Medals

Foreign orders and medals have, of course, always been popular abroad and they are now attracting a considerable amount of attention in Great Britain too. This is illustrated by the steady increase in the prices of foreign decorations in auction over the past years. A number of these awards have been, and are still, given to British recipients, this being particularly so during the Great War 1914-18. Many groups of British medals are found containing French, Imperial Russian, Belgian, Italian and Serbian awards. Two particularly attractive foreign Orders are shown in Figs.39 and 40.

Some of the existing European Orders of Chivalry are very old, for example the Danish Order of the Elephant (founded in 1642), the Badge of the Order being a white enamelled gold elephant with a howdah studded with precious stones. Other early examples are the Swedish Most Noble Order of the Seraphim, instituted in 1748, and the Portuguese Order of the Tower and the Sword (1459). A group of three medals containing this rare decoration, the Peninsular Gold Cross with two bars and a Large Army Gold Medal with one bar, to the Peninsular War veteran Lieutenant-General Sir William Stewart, sold in auction recently for £26,000.

The famous Legion of Honour of France was founded in 1802 by Napoleon Bonaparte, who recognised the need to reward his troops for brave conduct. There are five grades of the Order, Grand Cross, Grand Officer, Commander, Officer and Knight. The Legion is also given to foreigners for both military and civil service, and groups of medals to British recipients often include this honour from the Crimean War (1854-55) to the present. Another medal which is found among awards to British N.C.O.s is the Military Medal (*Medaille Militaire*) founded in 1852 by Napoleon

Fig. 40   Serbian Order of St. Sava

III. Early awards to British soldiers for the Crimean War are most desirable, the medal given during this period bearing the old French Imperial Eagle. The War Cross (*Croix de Guerre*) was instituted in 1915 as a decoration to represent a Mention in Dispatches. Additional bronze stars or palms were added to the ribbon to denote further awards and there have again been many British holders of this medal.

The German Iron Cross is a well-known decoration and was originally awarded in two Classes, 1st (pin-back type) and 2nd (with ribbon). This decoration was instituted in 1813 and reconstituted in 1870, 1914 and 1939. During the Second World War the Iron Cross was extended into four higher Classes, these being the Knights Cross of the Iron Cross; the same with Oak Leaves; again with Oak Leaves and Swords; and the highest grade, with Oak Leaves, Swords and Diamonds. A special award of the Knights Cross with Gold Oak Leaves, Swords and Diamonds was given to the 'tank-busting' ace Colonel Hans Ulrich Rudel, who was credited with destroying over 500 Russian tanks from the air. Another special award, the Grand Cross of the Order, was awarded to Field Marshal Goering following the fall of France in 1940. The War Cross of Merit (three Degrees) and the German Cross in Gold and Silver were also given for outstanding civil and military services to Germany during the war.

Another interesting series of awards which are peculiarly German are the 'war badges' given to German and auxiliary forces. There were a number of these, each arm of the Services having its own type, e.g. the Infantry Assault Badge (Army), the Destroyer War Badge (Navy) and the Pilot-Observer Badge (Air Force). These pin-on Badges (Fig.41) had to be earned in actual combat against the enemy over a period of time. Some have additional numbered plaques showing further engagements; the Tank Battle Badge, for example is found in four additional Classes, with the numbers '25', '50', '75' or '100' representing the number of tank battles the recipient took part in.

There is a great demand for German World War II militaria at present, especially for all the decorations and medals described. Great care must be taken when buying these awards, however, as numerous fakes and re-strikes exist, many taken from the dies from which the original decorations were struck. A very useful book on the subject is *Orders, Decorations, Medals and Badges of the Third Reich* by David Littlejohn and Colonel C. M. Dodkins.

29

Japanese decorations include the Order of the Rising Sun (established in 1876 in eight Classes) and the Order of the Sacred Treasure (1888). These awards are sometimes found with their original attractive wooden lacquered presentation boxes. Decorations to Europeans, with the original presentation scrolls, are scarce and well worth collecting.

Medals and decorations from the United States are gaining in popularity, especially the Congressional Medal of Honor, the American equivalent of the Victoria Cross. There are two types of this high award, one for the Army and Air Force, the other for the U.S. Navy. These rare medals rarely come on the market, but unnamed (unissued) examples occasionally become available. Named gallantry decorations such as the Distinguished Service Cross and Distinguished Service Medal are not common, and are seldom offered for sale. Verified awards to British recipients are very interesting additions to medal groups, most of these being given for service with United States units during the Second World War and the Korean War. Unnamed examples of other decorations, such as the Distinguished Flying

Fig. 41 German Destroyer
War Badge, 1939-45

Cross, the Air Medal, Bronze Star and Purple Heart, together with various modern campaign medals are often available, and an attractive and very reasonably priced collection can be made of them.

Housing a Collection

There are various ways to house a medal collection, the most attractive being in glazed wooden frames which are screwed to the wall. These frames are usually sold with felt backing, the medals being pinned to the backing by drawing pins. A neat way of doing this is to cut a small piece of cardboard, slightly narrower than the width of the ribbon, push the drawing pin through the cardboard and ribbon, and turn the ribbon over. The medal can then be pinned to the backing board with the pin and card concealed behind the ribbon. Details of the medal or medals, showing the recipient's name and regiment or ship, can be typewritten or printed on a small card and pinned below each medal or group with small-head map pins. Wall frames are also the best way to display groups of medals mounted on ribbon bars, as the long ribbon pin can be hooked over two or three drawing pins pushed well into the backing board. Neck badges and breast stars of Orders of Knighthood again look very attractive when mounted up in glazed frames, with details and perhaps photographs included in the frame with the awards.

Unfortunately there are two main drawbacks to displaying medals and orders in this way. As the value of medals steadily increases, so does the risk of theft. The actual frames can also be rather expensive as they are usually made of mahogany or oak. A cheaper variety has now appeared on the market made from pine which has been stained and varnished to appear like mahogany.

An alternative method of storage is in wooden cabinets containing a number of trays, the medals being laid flat in these on felt backing. Care must be taken to see that the trays are deep enough to take not only medals with their bars but also decorations and orders, especially Neck Badges and Breast Stars. Lockable metal cabinets can also be bought with quite deep drawers (about $\frac{3}{4}$ inch) from office stationery shops, but these must be lined with felt to prevent the medals being marked. Reasonably priced plastic coin cabinets have also appeared on the market which have special trays for 'crown size' coins, and these can be easily converted to take medals. The trays are already lined and thick plastic sheets can be bought to cover the trays, thus preventing the medal ribbons from lifting up when the trays are removed from the cabinets. The cabinets can be stacked on top of each other, and are ideal for storing cheaper medals, e.g. 1914-15 Star trios. They are not usually deep enough for mounted groups or orders.

Another method of storage is in plastic medal pouches which take both medal and ribbon; these are ideal when the medals are frequently handled. The pouches can be kept in special medal albums that have plastic leaves which hold six medals in pouches to a page, so that up to fifty-four medals can be kept in an album. The albums will take all standard-size campaign medals and decorations, but not mounted groups or orders. Whichever method is chosen, care should be taken to see that medals are not kept in direct contact with each other, especially bronze stars and silver medals, as this can cause contact marking and scratching and, in the case of orders, enamel chipping and flaking.

Detection of Fakes

A most important point to consider in medal collecting is the identification of fakes and copies, also the so-called 'renamed' medals. Fortunately there are not many fakes of British medals about, but re-engraving of the recipient's name and regiment or ship on the edge of campaign medals is something the collector must always be aware of. This was usually done in the early days by a soldier or sailor who had lost his original medal and needed a replacement. He therefore bought another medal, usually from a pawnbroker, with the bars he was entitled to, had the original recipient's name taken off and his own engraved thereon. These renamed medals can be detected, as the rim section where the original name has been removed has a filed-down appearance. The medal is also no longer a perfectly round disc and this can be confirmed by taking measurements around the rim with calipers or an engineer's micrometer screw gauge. Another indication is that the medals are usually engraved in a different style of lettering from that used on the medal when originally issued. The reason so much emphasis is placed on the importance of identifying renamed medals is that the value is considerably affected by this alteration, sometimes reducing the value of a medal to scrap value only. It should be pointed out though that, on some rare occasions, medals are found officially renamed, but these should always be verified and accompanied by a guarantee of authenticity from the seller. A very useful book which illustrates the different types of naming on campaign medals and gives details of other copies and fakes is *Collecting Medals and Decorations* by Alec Purves.

There are campaign medals, such as the early Afghan medals and the Crimean issues, that were officially issued unnamed, but are sometimes found named up to deceive collectors. This has been done to make the medal more valuable, for example in the case where a medal was given to men who were present at a famous action. The same intent also applies to the bars on a medal; if added to or subtracted from it, this sometimes causes a dramatic increase in the value. The best way to check whether a man is entitled to a medal and bars, where issued, is against the Medal Roll. These rolls were drawn up prior to the issue of a medal and show a man's entitlement. These rolls and supporting documents can be studied at the Public Record Office, though a Reader's Ticket is necessary for this. Printed medal rolls for different regiments are sometimes produced; for example Don Forsyth of South Africa has published the complete roll for the South Africa Medal 1877-79.

An alternative method of verification is to use the services of an expert. There are a number of collectors and dealers who can arrange to do this for a small fee. The best way, however, to build up a genuine medal collection is to buy from recognised medal dealers and auction houses who will guarantee that medals bought from them are genuine, and who will give an immediate refund should the item later prove to be incorrect in any way.

It is always advisable to keep a record of the medal collection, either in a loose-leaf book or on a filing card system. This can be a very useful record for insurance purposes, and additional interesting information can be added concerning the action or campaign for which the medals were given. All documents and photographs bought with a medal should be carefully filed, and passed on with the medal when it is sold, as often these documents cannot be replaced.

Reference Works

Apart from the books already mentioned, there are some basic reference works of great importance to the medal collector. Suggested books are: *The Standard Catalogue of British Orders, Decorations and Medals*, a priced catalogue by E. C. Joslin; *Ribbons and Medals*, H. Taprell Dorling and L. G. Guille; *British Battles and Medals*, Major L. L. Gordon; and *British Gallantry Awards*, P. E. Abbott and J. M. A. Tamplin. A useful and very reasonably priced little book is *The Observer's Book of British Awards and Medals*, again by E. C. Joslin. Books on foreign medals include *Orders, Medals and Decorations of Britain and Europe*, P. Hieronymussen; *Military Medals and Decorations*, Yves Arden; *Book of Orders and Decorations*, Vaclav Mericka; and *American War Medals and Decorations*, Evans E. Kerrigan.

Other medal books can be added later as the need arises, and there is, of course, a vast amount of literature available on the various campaigns and wars for which medals have been awarded. An interesting sideline can also be made of early books on medals, such as George Tancred's *Historical Records of Medals and Honorary Distinctions* (1891) and Thomas Carter's *Medals of the British Army*, published in three volumes in 1861.

The collector should also seriously consider joining the Orders and Medals Research Society. This first-class organisation holds regular monthly meetings at its London headquarters and issues a very informative quarterly Journal, which helps members who live outside London and those abroad to keep in touch with developments in medal collecting. The Society holds two medal auctions a year for its members and there is a well-attended annual Congress. Membership details can be supplied by any of the large London medal dealers.